Welcome to the **EVERYTHING® series!**

These handy, accessible books give you all you need to tackle a difficult project, gain a new hobby, comprehend a fascinating topic, prepare for an exam, or even brush up on something you learned back in school but have since forgotten.

You can read an *EVERYTHING®* book from cover to cover or just pick out the information you want. We literally give you everything you need to know on the subject, but throw in a lot of fun stuff along the way, too.

We now have well over 300 *EVERYTHING®* books in print, spanning such wide-ranging topics as weddings, pregnancy, wine, learning guitar, one-pot cooking, managing people, and so much more. When you're done reading them all, you can finally say you know *EVERYTHING®*!

Dear Reader,

You probably bought this book in hopes of learning more about your IQ and intelligence in general. In the United States, intelligence testing has come up against more negative publicity than in just about any other country in the world, leaving many adults with only a vague idea of where they stand intelligence-wise.

I wrote this book not only to help those who are curious about their IQ take several tests to determine their range of intelligence, but also to provide resources and additional information about IQ testing and intelligence. I've endeavored to create a comprehensive collection of tests that cover the entire spectrum of modern intelligence testing.

It's a good idea not to put too much stock in a single score, however, because while someone with a high IQ does have an advantage in life, it no more guarantees success than a low IQ guarantees failure.

Nathan Haselbauer

THE
EVERYTHING®
TEST YOUR
IQ
BOOK

Discover your true intelligence

Nathan Haselbauer

A

Adams Media
Avon, Massachusetts

An Everything® Series Book.
Everything® and everything.com® are registered trademarks of
F+W Publications, Inc.

Published by Adams Media, an F+W Publications Company
57 Littlefield Street, Avon, MA 02322 U.S.A.
www.adamsmedia.com

ISBN: 1-59337-437-2

Printed in Canada.

J I H G F E D C B A

Library of Congress Cataloging-in-Publication Data
Haselbauer, Nathan.
The everything test your IQ book : discover your
true intelligence / Nathan Haselbauer.
p. cm. -- (An everything series book)
ISBN 1-59337-437-2
1. Intelligence tests. 2. Self-evaluation. I. Title: Test your
IQ book. II. Title. III. Series: Everything series.

BF431.3.H37 2005
153.9'3--dc20

2005026453

This publication is designed to provide accurate and authoritative information with regard to the subject matter covered. It is sold with the understanding that the publisher is not engaged in rendering legal, accounting, or other professional advice. If legal advice or other expert assistance is required, the services of a competent professional person should be sought.

—From a *Declaration of Principles* jointly adopted by a Committee of the American Bar Association and a Committee of Publishers and Associations

Many of the designations used by manufacturers and sellers to distinguish their products are claimed as trademarks. Where those designations appear in this book and Adams Media was aware of a trademark claim, the designations have been printed with initial capital letters.

This book is available at quantity discounts for bulk purchases.
For information, please call 1-800-872-5627.

THE

EVERYTHING

Series

EDITORIAL

Publishing Director: Gary M. Krebs

Associate Managing Editor: Laura M. Daly

Associate Copy Chief: Brett Palana-Shanahan

Acquisitions Editor: Gina Chaimanis

Development Editor: Meredith O'Hayre

Associate Production Editor: Casey Ebert

PRODUCTION

Director of Manufacturing: Susan Beale

Associate Director of Production: Michelle Roy Kelly

Cover Design: Paul Beatrice,

Erick DaCosta, and Matt LeBlanc

Design and Layout: Colleen Cunningham,

Holly Curtis, Sorae Lee

Series Cover Artist: Barry Littmann

Visit the entire Everything® series at www.everything.com

This book is dedicated to all the people out there who have never stopped learning.

• • •

Acknowledgments

This book wouldn't have been possible without support from the members of the International High IQ Society who were the testing ground, making these tests as accurate and informative as possible.

Contents

A Note to the Reader

After each test in this book, you'll find the following paragraph:

It's important to keep in mind that since this test is not given under controlled conditions and has not gone through rigorous standardizing and normalization, it cannot give a true IQ score. The score given on this test is merely meant to be an indicator of how you might perform on an IQ test. Your obtained score should only be interpreted as a broad estimate of your intelligence.

Because of the limitations of the printed form, the tests in this book cannot be as accurate as a professional IQ test administered by a licensed psychologist. For adults, the gold standard in IQ testing is the Wechsler Adult Intelligence Scale (WAIS). The WAIS is now on its third version and is generally considered to be the most thorough test available. Unfortunately, it can be cumbersome to find a local psychologist who is willing to administer it and the costs can be substantial. They range from $200 all the way up to $500, depending on where you live.

Great strides have been made in online testing, which may offer you a more affordable approach to IQ testing.

The proliferation of online IQ tests spurred the American Psychological Association (APA) to put together an ad hoc committee called the Task Force for Psychological Testing on the Internet. The APA's Board of Scientific Affairs and Board of Professional Affairs established the task force in 2001 to inform psychologists about the state of Internet testing. Their findings show that there are some functional, fair and reliable tests online, provided they follow the basic principles of reliability and validity.

I have spent several years designing and norming various intelligence tests and have taken concepts from this book as well as features not available to the print form (such as questions weighted by the time it takes you to answer them) and developed an online test for the International High IQ Society. The test can be found at *www.highiqsociety.org* and it incorporates many features of professional intelligence tests, yet can be taken online free of charge.

Introduction

Many psychologists believe IQ tests predict academic and vocational success with moderate efficiency. However, they are not intended to measure other important variables such as abilities responsible for art, music, cooking, mechanical invention, foreign languages, caring for a baby, defeating an enemy in war, and so on. In addition, all professional IQ tests have a degree of error derived from thorough statistical analyses of the standardization sample. It's important to keep in mind that since the tests in this book are not given under controlled conditions and have not gone through rigorous standardizing and normalization, they cannot give a true IQ score. The scores given on our tests are merely meant to be an indicator of how a person might perform on an IQ test. In short, your obtained score should only be interpreted as a broad estimate of your intelligence.

The world of intelligence testing is one of ongoing debate. Modern psychology has refined the intelligence test to a degree never thought possible even fifty years ago, yet there are still numerous detractors who make blanket dismissals about the current state of intelligence testing.

What's interesting to note is that the large majority of those who criticize the notion of IQ testing are not professionals in the field, but journalists, book reviewers, television personalities, and others in the media who have no expert knowledge in this field. In Snyderman and Rothman's book *The IQ Controversy*, the authors questioned more than 600 of the leading experts in all fields of modern psychometric testing and they found almost universal agreement amongst the professionals about what IQ tests measure and their value in assessing intelligence.

Chapter 1
The General
IQ Test

This test measures several factors of intelligence, including spatial ability, logical reasoning, and verbal and mathematical skills. There are forty questions to answer with a time limit of forty-five minutes. Most people will not finish the test, so don't rush through it just to get to the end. You may use a calculator, a piece of paper, and a pencil.

Number of questions: 40
Time limit: 45 minutes

START TEST

1. Complete the sequence.

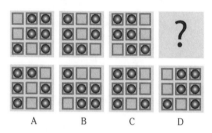

2. If Pittsford is closer to Mendon than Brighton, and Mendon is closer to Pittsford than Brighton, then Brighton is closer to:

   A. Pittsford
   B. Mendon
   C. Impossible to tell

3. On Tuesday, Craig rode his bicycle half as fast as he normally does, and twice as fast as he did last Sunday. If Craig normally bicycles 20 kilometers per hour, how many kilometers per hour did he bicycle last Sunday?

   A. 2
   B. 5
   C. 10
   D. 20
   E. Cannot be determined

4. When filled completely with water, which of these 2 cubes would hold the most liquid?

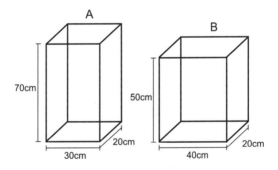

   A. Cube A would hold the most.
   B. Cube B would hold the most.
   C. Both cubes would hold an identical amount.

5. Which of the following words is closest in meaning to METICULOUS?

   A. Fastidious
   B. Slipshod
   C. Unwitting
   D. Thoughtless

6. Which of the following words is closest in meaning to VITUPERATION?

   A. Adulation
   B. Laudation
   C. Vilification
   D. Admiration

7. Complete the sequence.

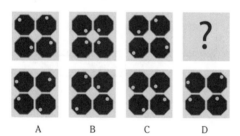

A   B   C   D

8. The local butcher sells steak on Mondays for 50 percent off and chicken on Thursdays for 40 percent off. If chicken is normally $2.50 per pound and steak is normally $3 per pound, then which is cheaper: a pound of chicken on Thursdays or a pound of steak on Mondays?

   A. The steak.
   B. The chicken.
   C. Both are the same price.

9. The opposite of ACCLIMATE is?

   A. Conform
   B. Disturb
   C. Familiarize
   D. Adapt

10. The opposite of HETEROGENEOUS is?

   A. Disparate
   B. Varied
   C. Incongruous
   D. Identical

11. Complete the sequence: 13, 17, 31, 37, 71, 73, 79, 97, 107, _____.

12. Finish the following list of even numbers: 2, 4, 6, 30, 32, 34, 36, 40, 42, 44, _____?

13. Which of the following words is closest in meaning to FALLIBLE?

    A. Righteous
    B. Correct
    C. Imperfect
    D. Unerring

14. Complete the sequence.

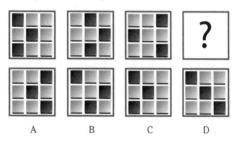

A   B   C   D

15. The local factory's workforce is 20 percent part-time workers, with the rest of the workers full-time. At the end of the year, 30 percent of the full-time workers received bonuses. If 72 full-time workers received bonuses, how many workers does the factory employ?

16. Find the missing box.

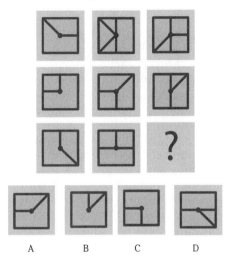

A   B   C   D

17. Find the missing number: 6000, 3000, _____, 750, 325.

18. Tarbs are twice as long as Gobs. Wobbles are 3 times as long as Tarbs. That means:

    A. Gobs are 6 times as long as Wobbles.
    B. Wobbles are 8 times as long as Gobs.
    C. Gobs are 8 times as long as Wobbles.
    D. Wobbles are 6 times as long as Gobs.

19. There is a system of pricing at the ice cream store. How much should the mocha cost?

$$
\begin{array}{rr}
\text{CHERRY} & 13 \\
\text{VANILLA} & 17 \\
\text{CHOCOLATE} & 22 \\
\text{STRAWBERRY} & 22 \\
\text{MOCHA} & ?
\end{array}
$$

20. Which of the two interior squares is bigger?

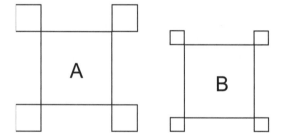

   A. Square A is larger.
   B. Square B is larger.
   C. Both A and B are identical in size.

21. Can the word TROOPER be spelled using only the letters found in the word OBSTREPEROUS?

22. The following sentence makes sense if the word "beuss" is understood to mean the same as the word "play." Even though some of the beussers had never beussed before, they all did their best to beuss as hard as they could.

23. Can the word SILLINESS be spelled by using the first letters of the words in the following sentence: Several intelligent liars love instigating negatively ethical sad standards.

24. If written backward, would the number, "nine thousand, three hundred and twelve," be written, "two thousand, one hundred and thirty-nine"?

25. Which of the following rectangles is on top of the rest?

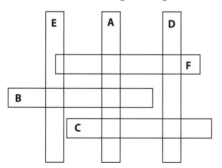

26. Do the words MOUNTAINEERS, ENUMERATIONS, and RENOMINATES all use the exact same letters?

27. Is the fifteenth vowel appearing in this sentence the letter E?

28. If the word ZOOM is written under the word CARS and the word ABLE is written under the word ZOOM and the word ACID is written under the word ABLE then the word COLD is formed diagonally.

29. Change the first letter of each word pair to form new words, then place the new first letter between the parentheses to form a new word vertically.

    Example: LAND ( ) MEAL becomes SAND (S) SEAL and the S is placed in the parentheses.

    MEAL ( ) TIDE
    GEAR ( ) SICK
    CAT ( ) OTHER
    ODD ( ) ICE
    POST ( ) FINE

30. Grabes are twice as tall as Rebes. Saters are 4 times as tall as Grabes. That means:

    A. Grabes are 6 times as tall as Saters.
    B. Saters are 8 times as tall as Rebes.
    C. Rebes are 4 times as tall as Grabes.
    D. Saters are 4 times as tall as Rebes.

31. Five pros and 13 cons can build 576 neutrals in 9 hours, and 8 cons and 3 pros can build 546 neutrals in 14 hours. At what rate do pros and cons build neutrals? Express your answers in neutrals per hour.

32. RECENT and PERCENT are:

    A. Similar
    B. Dissimilar
    C. Opposite

33. In which image is the line the longest?

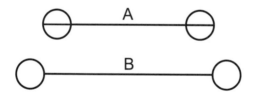

34. ZIPPER is to COAT as LOCK is to:

    A. Paper
    B. Walking
    C. Door
    D. Food
    E. Shoe

35. All spinners are handles and most handles are fun. Most handles are fish, therefore some spinners are fish.

    A. True
    B. False
    C. Indeterminable from data given

36. Can the word CERTIFY be spelled using only the letters found in the word ELECTRICITY?

37. Complete the sequence and find the missing box.

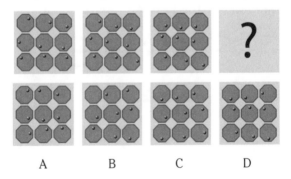

A   B   C   D

38. Complete the sequence and find the missing box.

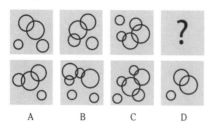

A   B   C   D

39. Oop nostrum signi means "You eat lead."
    Nostrem ingblot inx means "How you read."
    Ogslim inx blit means "How are fireworks."
    What words would you use to say: "How are you?"
    The order that you place the words in is unimport-
    ant—you only need to find the correct words to use.

40. If the word NECK is written above the word SALT, and
    the word SALT is written above the word BLIP and the
    word TAIL is written underneath the word BLIP, then
    the word NAIL is formed diagonally.

END TEST

ANSWER KEY

1. D
2. C
3. B
4. A
5. A
6. C
7. B
8. C
9. B
10. D
11. 113. Primes whose reversal is a different prime.
12. 46. The letter E is banned in all the numbers.
13. C
14. C
15. 300. Twenty percent of the workers are part-time, so 80 percent of the workers are full-time. Thirty percent received bonuses and this amounted to 72 workers. Thirty percent of 80 percent of total workers (n) equals 72. $3/10 \times 8/10 \times n = 72$, or $24/100 \times n = 72$. Therefore, $n = 72 \times 100/24$ or 300.
16. D
17. 1500. Divide each number by two.
18. D
19. 12
20. C
21. Yes
22. True
23. Yes

24. Yes
25. C
26. No
27. Yes
28. Yes
29. S T E A L
    MEAL (S) TIDE
    GEAR (T) SICK
    CAT (E) OTHER
    ODD (A) ICE
    POST (L) FINE
30. B
31. Pros build at 5 neutrals per hour and cons build at 3 neutrals per hour.
32. B
33. Both A and B are the same size.
34. C
35. A
36. No
37. D
38. C
39. Ogslim inx nostrum.
40. Yes

Interpreting Your Score

The following chart will convert your raw score into your estimated IQ score. Simply calculate the number of questions you answered correctly (your raw score) and match it up with the corresponding logic IQ score on the right.

Raw score   IQ rate

A	B
0	<70
1	70
2	72
3	74
4	76
5	78
6	80
7	82
8	84
9	86
10	88
11	90
12	92

13	94
14	96
15	98
16	100
17	102
18	104
19	106
20	108
21	110
22	112
23	114
24	116
25	118
26	120

27	122
28	124
29	126
30	128
31	130
32	132
33	134
34	136
35	138
36	140
37	142
38	144
39	146
40	150+

It's important to keep in mind that since this test is not given under controlled conditions, and has not gone through rigorous standardizing and normalization, it cannot give a true IQ score. The score given on this test is merely meant to be an indicator of how you might perform on an IQ test. Your obtained score should only be interpreted as a broad estimate of your intelligence.

Chapter 2
Culture-Fair Intelligence Test

The culture-fair intelligence test is designed to test IQ while minimizing cultural and educational biases. This test relies on pictures and images rather than words, and primarily assesses your spatial abilities. The concept of spatial ability consists of several components, such as mental rotation, spatial perception, and spatial visualization.

This test features two sets of questions, analog matrices and sequential matrices. They require you to find the pattern in the images and find the box that best completes the pattern. While some may seem simple, there are several "red herrings" in the questions that are designed to purposely distract the test-taker. Finding the correct pattern and extrapolating it to the blank square can get quite tricky.

Number of questions: 25
Time limit: 45 minutes

START TEST

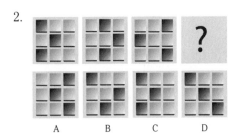

3.

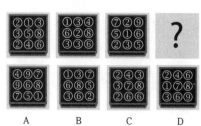

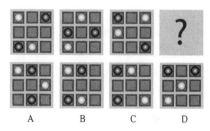

4.

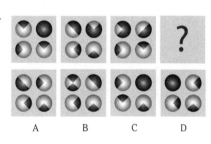

5.

6.

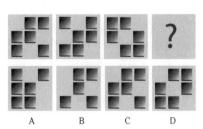

A   B   C   D

7.

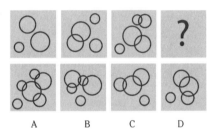

A   B   C   D

8.

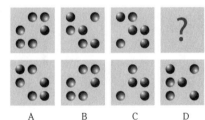

A   B   C   D

9.

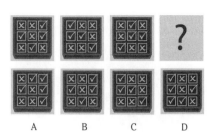

A   B   C   D

10.

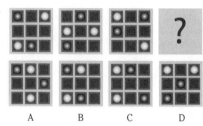

A   B   C   D

11.

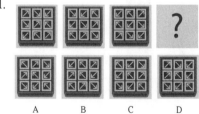

A   B   C   D

12.

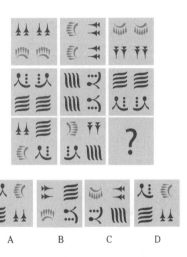

13.

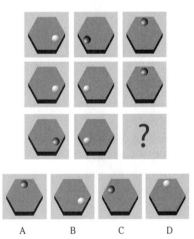

14.

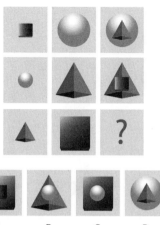

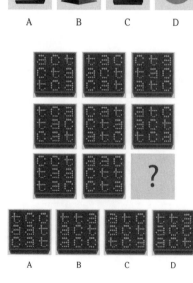

A B C D

15.

A B C D

16.

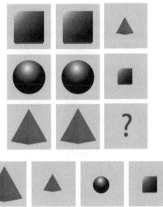

17.

18.

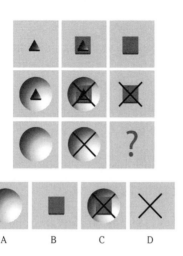

19.

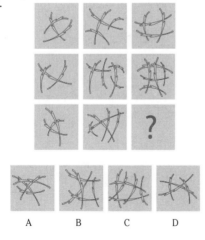

20.

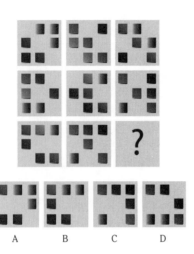

21.

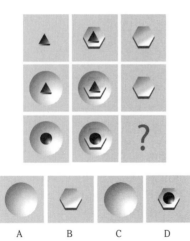

22.

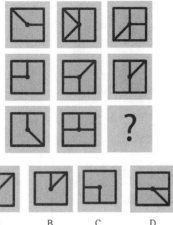

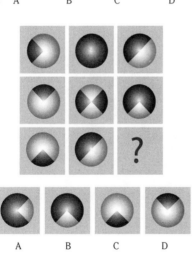

23.

24.

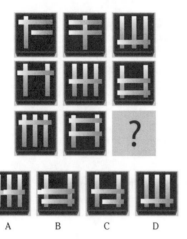

25.

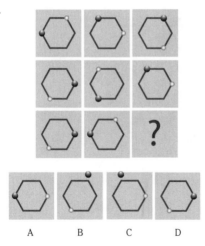

END TEST

ANSWER KEY

1. A
2. C
3. D
4. D
5. A
6. C
7. B
8. B
9. B
10. A
11. A
12. D
13. D
14. C
15. D
16. C
17. D
18. D
19. C
20. A
21. B
22. D
23. A
24. A
25. D

Interpreting Your Score

The chart below will convert your raw score into your estimated IQ score. Simply calculate the number of questions you answered correctly (your raw score) and match it up with the corresponding IQ score on the right.

Raw score	IQ rate
0	<70
1	72
2	76
3	80
4	84
5	88
6	92
7	96
8	100
9	104
10	108
11	110
12	112
13	116
14	118
15	120
16	123
17	126
18	130
19	134
20	138
21	140
22	142
23	144
24	146
25	150+

It's important to keep in mind that since this test is not given under controlled conditions and has not gone through rigorous standardizing and normalization, it cannot give a true IQ score. The score given on this test is merely meant to be an indicator of how you might perform on an IQ test. Your obtained score should only be interpreted as a broad estimate of your intelligence.

Chapter 3
Verbal Intelligence Test

Verbal intelligence is essentially the ability to use words and language. Those possessing a strong verbal intelligence tend to have highly developed skills for reading, speaking, and writing. This test is designed for those whose first language is English. Take your time, read the questions carefully and choose the best response. Pencil and paper are allowed, but use of any reference material such as a dictionary, encyclopedia, or thesaurus is not allowed.

Number of questions: 40
Time limit: 45 minutes

START TEST

1. Can the word GENERAL be spelled using only the letters found in the word ENLARGEMENT?

2. Can the word HUTCH be spelled by using the first letters of the words in the following sentence: He used to call her?

3. If written backward, would the number, "nineteen thousand, four hundred and eighty-one," be written, "eighteen thousand, four hundred and ninety-one"?

4. The following sentence makes sense if the word "telb" is understood to mean the same as the word "drink." Many telbers feel that telbing makes them smarter so they must continue to telb often.

5. Do the words CARTER, CATER, and CARET all use the exact same letters?

6. Is the eighteenth vowel appearing in this sentence the letter I?

7. In the English alphabet, how many letters are there between the letter B and the letter Z?

8. If the word PLAY is written under the word BURN and the word NOUN is written under the word PLAY and the word NOTE is written under the word NOUN then the word BLUR is formed diagonally.

9. If you remove nine letters from the word EXTERMINATED, can the word TIME be formed?

10. Is the following sentence spelled the same forwards as it is backward? Anna is Anna.

11. Do the vowels in the word ANTERIORLY appear in alphabetical order?

12. Change the first letter of each word pair to form new words, then place the new first letter between the parentheses to form a new word vertically.

Example: FAR ( ) RAT becomes CAR ( ) CAT and the C is placed in the parentheses.

SLOT ( ) CLAY
MOOSE ( ) SETTER
GEL ( ) CAR
ORE ( ) NEON
LAND ( ) MEAL
SIDE ( ) KIDS
FEAR ( ) RAIL
EACH ( ) POWER

13. Which of the following words is closest in meaning to APPREHENSIVE?

    A. Thorough
    B. Foolish
    C. Anxious
    D. Distraught

14. Mord are 3 times as long as Romd. Drom are twice as long as Mord. That means:

    A. Mord are 6 times as long as Drom.
    B. Drom are 8 times as tall as Romd.
    C. Mord are 4 times as tall as Drom.
    D. Drom are 6 times as tall as Romd.

15. Bloc dop zipo means "Fine art teacher."
    Foo oobleck nitz eck means "A walrus am I."
    Zipo toc brin oobleck means "I have fine furniture."
    What words would you use to say: "I am fine?" The order that you place the words in is unimportant—you only need to find the correct words to use.

16. All Motr are Prok and no Motr are Rta, so the statement that some Prok are Rta is:

    A. True
    B. False
    C. Indeterminable from data given

17. PERCEPTUAL and SCULPTURAL are:

    A. Similar
    B. Dissimilar
    C. Opposite

18. HAMBURGER is to MAN as GRASS is to:

    A. Bicycle
    B. Ship
    C. Computer
    D. Sheep
    E. Winter

19. All Nerds are Jerks and some Nerds are Geeks. All Geeks are BrainMasters, therefore all BrainMasters are Jerks.

    A. True
    B. False
    C. Indeterminable from data given

20. Can the word NOMINAL be spelled using only the letters found in the word NATURALIZATION?

21. Can the word FORWARD be spelled by using the first letters of the words in the following sentence: Fight or riot when a rabbit dies.

22. If written backward, would the number, "forty-one thousand, seven hundred and twenty-six," be written, "sixty-two thousand, seven hundred and forty-one"?

23. The following sentence makes sense if the word "dolk" is understood to mean the same as the word "hunt." Some dolkers are addicted to dolking despite the fact that the dolk could be in danger of extinction.

24. Do the words ALERTING, INTEGRAL, RELATING, and TRIANGLE all use the exact same letters?

25. Is the tenth vowel appearing in this sentence the letter I?

26. In the English alphabet, how many letters are there between the letter E and the letter T?

27. If the word SILO is written under the word KISS and the word PAST is written above the word PERK and the word SILO is written above the word PAST then the word SLAP is formed diagonally.

28. If you remove 8 letters from the word INFLATIONARY, can the word RIOT be formed?

29. Reas are 5 times as big as Steers. Coos are 8 times as big as Reas. That means:

    A. Reas are 40 times as large as Coos.
    B. Reas are 50 times as large as Coos.
    C. Coos are 40 times as large as Steers.
    D. Coos are 50 times as large as Steers.

30. All Radom are Rokr and most Radom are Tork, so the statement that some Rokr are Tork is:

    A. True
    B. False
    C. Indeterminable from data given

31. PENNY is to DOLLAR as PROVINCE is to:

    A. State
    B. City
    C. Country
    D. Moon
    E. Pocketbook

32. Some Serps are Trags and most Serps are Prens. Some Prens are Tacres, therefore a few Tacres are Trags.

    A. True
    B. False
    C. Indeterminable from data given

33. Can the word STRANGE be spelled using only the letters found in the word TRANSGRESSION?

34. The following sentence makes sense if the word "bleg" is understood to mean the same as the word "invent." The famous blegger, Thomas A. Edison, blegged countless blegs that he blegged.

35. Do the words REPAINT, PAINTER, and PERTAIN all use the exact same letters?

36. Is the fourth consonant from the end of this sentence an N?

37. In the English alphabet, how many letters are there between the letter F and the letter L?

38. If you remove 6 letters from the word ADMIRALTIES, can the word SLIME be formed?

39. If most fannies are balrogs and some balrogs are monsters, the statement that most fannies are monsters is:

    A. True
    B. False
    C. Indeterminable from data given

40. LIGHT BULB is to FILAMENT as WHEEL is to:

    A. Electricity
    B. Road
    C. Spoke
    D. Automobile
    E. Pulley

END TEST

ANSWER KEY

1. Yes
2. Yes
3. Yes
4. Yes
5. No
6. No
7. 23
8. No
9. No
10. No
11. Yes
12. P L E A S A N T
    SLOT (P) CLAY
    MOOSE (L) SETTER
    GEL (E) CAR
    ORE (A) NEON
    LAND (S) MEAL
    SIDE (A) KIDS
    FEAR (N) RAIL
    LEACH (T) POWER
13. C
14. D
15. Eck zipo oobleck.
16. C
17. B
18. D
19. B
20. No

21. Yes
22. No
23. No
24. Yes
25. Yes
26. 14
27. No
28. Yes
29. C
30. A
31. C
32. A
33. Yes
34. No
35. Yes
36. Yes
37. 5
38. Yes
39. C
40. C

Interpreting Your Score

The following chart will convert your raw score into your estimated verbal IQ score. Simply calculate the number of questions you answered correctly (your raw score) and match it up with the corresponding IQ score on the right.

Raw score   IQ rate

A	B
0	<70
1	70
2	72
3	74
4	76
5	78
6	80
7	82
8	84
9	86
10	88
11	90
12	92

13	94
14	96
15	98
16	100
17	102
18	104
19	106
20	108
21	110
22	112
23	114
24	116
25	118
26	120

27	122
28	124
29	126
30	128
31	130
32	132
33	134
34	136
35	138
36	140
37	142
38	144
39	146
40	150+

It's important to keep in mind that since this test is not given under controlled conditions and has not gone through rigorous standardizing and normalization, it cannot give a true IQ score. The score given on this test is merely meant to be an indicator of how you might perform on an IQ test. Your obtained score should only be interpreted as a broad estimate of your intelligence.

Chapter 4
Logical Intelligence Test

L ogical intelligence is our ability to mentally process logical problems and equations, the type most often found on multiple choice standardized tests. Of all the different types of intelligences, this one is the most thoroughly documented and studied.

This intelligence test uses numbers, math, and logic to arrive at the correct answer. If you happen to be a logical mathematically inclined person, you tend to think more conceptually and abstractly and are often able to see patterns and relationships that others miss. People with a high level of this intelligence tend to enjoy solving puzzles, working with numbers and mathematical formulas, and the challenge of a complex problem to solve.

This test is designed to test your logic and mathematical IQ. It will assess your ability to solve mathematical and logic word problems and it does not require mathematical education above the high school level. You are permitted to use a calculator and a piece of paper and a pencil.

Number of questions: 20
Time limit: 45 minutes

START TEST

1. During the Little League baseball season, every team plays every other team in the league 10 times. If there are 10 teams in the league, how many games are played in the league in 1 season?

2. Two people can make 2 bicycles in 2 hours. How many people are needed to make 12 bicycles in 6 hours?

    A. 2
    B. 3
    C. 4
    D. 5
    E. 6

3. A store reduced the price of one of its products by 25 percent. What percentage of the reduced price must it be increased by to put the product back to its original price?

    A. 25 percent
    B. 30 percent
    C. 33 percent
    D. 50 percent
    E. 66 percent

4. A box contains 2 coins. One coin is heads on both sides and the other is heads on one side and tails on the other. 1 coin is selected from the box at random and the face of 1 side is observed. If the face is heads what is the percent chance that the other side is heads?

    A. 25 percent
    B. 33 percent
    C. 50 percent
    D. 66 percent
    E. 88 percent

5. There are a total of 10 bicycles and tricycles. If the total number of wheels is 24, how many are tricycles?

    A. 2
    B. 3
    C. 4
    D. 5
    E. 6

6. John bought a painting for $8,000. If he sells it for a profit of 12.5 percent of the original cost, what is the selling price of the painting?

    A. $8,125
    B. $8,800
    C. $9,000
    D. $9,500
    E. $10,000

7. A ship floats with 3/5 of its weight above the water. What is the ratio of the ship's submerged weight to its exposed weight?

    A. 3:8
    B. 2:5
    C. 3:5
    D. 2:3
    E. 5:3

8. Seven kips and 12 ligs can build 826 tors in 14 hours, and 9 kips and 9 ligs can build 567 tors in 9 hours. At what rates do kips and ligs build tors? Express your answer in tors per hour.

9. If most Gannucks are Dorks and some Gannucks are Xorgs, the statement that some Dorks are Xorgs is:

    A. True
    B. False
    C. Indeterminable from data given

10. Dan's weekly salary is $70 less than Jerry's, whose weekly salary is $50 more than Sally's. If Sally earns $280 per week, how much does Dan earn per week?

11. A certain book costs $12 more in hardcover than in softcover. If the softcover price is 2/3 of the hardcover price, how much does the book cost in hardcover?

12. An office has 27 employees. If there are 7 more women than men in the office, how many employees are women?

13. Eric has $100 more than Ron. After Eric spends $20 on groceries, Eric has 5 times as much money as Ron. How much money does Ron have?

14. There are enough gumballs in a bag to give 12 gumballs to each of the 20 children, with no gumballs left over. If 5 children do not want any gumballs, how many gumballs can be given to each of the others?

15. A subway car passes an average of 3 stations every 10 minutes. At this rate, how many stations will it pass in 1 hour?

16. The local factory's workforce is 20 percent part-time workers, with the rest of the workers full-time. At the end of the year 30 percent of the full-time workers received bonuses. If 72 full-time workers received bonuses, how many workers does the factory employ?

17. Two rival colleges decided to have a tug of war. From their starting positions College A pulls College B forward 3 meters, and are then pulled forward themselves 5 meters. College B then pulls College A forward 2 meters. If the first college to be pulled forward 10 meters loses, how many more meters must College B pull College A forward to win?

18. Jonathan finds that by wearing different combinations of the jackets, shirts, and pairs of pants that he owns, he can make up 90 different outfits. If he owns 5 jackets and 3 pairs of pants, how many shirts does he own?

19. A foghorn sounds regularly 5 times a minute. A neighboring foghorn blows regularly 4 times a minute. If they blow simultaneously, after how many seconds will they blow together again?

20. Alison owes Robert $4, Robert owes Christine $3, and Christine owes Alison $5. If Christine settles all the debts by giving money to both Alison and Robert, how much will she give Alison?

END TEST

ANSWER KEY

1. 450. In the 10-team league, each team plays the other
    9 teams 10 times each. 9 x 10 = 90 games per team per
    season. With 10 different teams, we arrive at 900 total
    games played. Then we divide this by 2 since there
    are 2 teams playing in each game. 900 divided by 2
    equals 450.

2. C

3. C

4. D

5. C

6. C

7. D

8. Kips build 5 tors per hour and ligs build 2 tors per
    hour.

9. C

10. $260. Sally makes $280. If Jerry makes $50 more than
    this, then Jerry must make $280 + $50 or $330. Dan
    makes $70 less than this amount, or $260.

11. $36

12. 17. You just need to find 2 numbers that are 7 apart
    that add up to 27. With trial and error you should be
    able to find them soon; 10 and 17; there must be 17
    women working at the office.

13. $20

14. 16. Find the total number of gumballs in the bag, then
    divide by the new number of children who will be
    sharing them.

15. 18 stations. The subway will pass 60/10 or 6 times as many stations in 1 hour as it passes in 10 minutes. In 10 minutes it passes 3 stations; in 60 minutes it must pass 6 x 3 or 18 stations.

16. 300. Twenty percent of the workers are part-time, so 80 percent of the workers are full-time. 30 percent received bonuses and this amounted to 72 workers. Thirty percent of 80 percent of total workers (n) equals 72. 3/10 x 8/10 x n = 72, or 24/100 x n = 72. Therefore, n = 72 x 100/24 or 300.

17. 6. Find out how far College A has moved thus far. They pulled College B forward 3 meters, so A moved backward 3 meters. Then they were pulled forward 5 meters and then a further 2 meters. In total then they have moved forward (-3) + 5 + 2 = 4 meters. They must be pulled a further 6 meters to be pulled 10 meters forward.

18. 6. For every pair of pants, he can wear 5 different jackets, giving 5 different combinations for each pair of pants, or 3 x 15 = 15 different combinations of pants and jackets. With each of these combinations he can wear any of his different shirts. The different combinations of shirts, jackets, and pants is (number of shirts) / 15. We are told this equals 90, so 90 divided by 15 equals 6.

19. 60. If you convert everything to seconds, the first foghorn blows every 12 seconds and the second foghorn blows every 15 seconds. Then find the lowest common denominator, which is 60, and you arrive at the answer.

20. $1. Christine is owed $3 by Robert, and she owes $5 to Alison. She needs a cash loss of $2 to settle all debts. Alison, on the other hand, is owed $5 by Christine

and owes $4 to Robert. She must have a gain of $1. Since Christine settles all debts, this $1 must come from Christine, and this is the answer.

Interpreting Your Score

The chart below will convert your raw score into your estimated logic IQ score. Simply calculate the number of questions you answered correctly (your raw score) and match it up with the corresponding logic IQ score on the right.

Raw score	IQ rate
1	90
2	94
3	98
4	100
5	102
6	106
7	108
8	112
9	114
10	118
11	120
12	124
13	128
14	130
15	134
16	137
17	138
18	140
19	142
20	144

It's important to keep in mind that since this test is not given under controlled conditions and has not gone through rigorous standardizing and normalization, it cannot give a true IQ score. The score given on this test is merely meant to be an indicator of how you might perform on an IQ test. Your obtained score should only be interpreted as a broad estimate of your intelligence.

Chapter 5
Mathematical Intelligence Test

Mathematical intelligence is the capacity to use numbers effectively and to reason well, and traditional IQ tests and achievement tests rely heavily on math questions. Those who excel in math tend to think conceptually in logical and numerical patterns and do well with tasks such as problem solving, handling long chains of reason to make local progressions, and performing complex mathematical calculations.

There are twenty-five questions dealing with all aspects of mathematical intelligence. The use of pencil and paper is allowed, but electronic devices such as calculators and computers are not, and your score will not be as accurate if they are used.

Number of questions: 25
Time limit: none

START TEST

1. What is the product of the least common multiple and the greatest common factor of 15 and 24?

   A. 30
   B. 90
   C. 180
   D. 360
   E. 540

2. 1.28 can also be expressed as:

   A. 1-1/3
   B. 32/25
   C. 128/256
   D. 16/12
   E. 49/37

3. Which of the following is less than 1/6?

   A. 0.1667
   B. 3/18
   C. 0.167
   D. 0.1666
   E. 8/47

4. Complete the sequence: 2, 3, 3, 5, 10, 13, 39, 43, 172, 177, _____.

5. Which of the following fractions is closest in value to the decimal 0.31?

   A. 5/16
   B. 11/32
   C. 1/4
   D. 3/8
   E. 7/16

6. Which of the following numbers is evenly divisible by 6?

   A. 106
   B. 124
   C. 138
   D. 146
   E. 152

7. Complete the sequence: 1, 3, 6, 10, 15, 21, 28, _____.

8. Find the missing number: 6000, 3000, _____, 750, 325.

9. Which of the following is not a prime number?

   A. 53
   B. 59
   C. 61
   D. 67
   E. 74

10. Complete the sequence: 13, 17, 31, 37, 71, 73, 79, 97, 107, _____.

11. What is the greatest integer that will divide evenly into both 36 and 54?

   A. 6
   B. 9
   C. 12
   D. 18
   E. 27

12. If the average of x and 9 is 7, then x equals:

    A. 3
    B. 5
    C. 6
    D. 7
    E. 9

13. Complete the sequence: 1, 1, 2, 3, 5, 8, 13, _____ .

14. In a certain pet store there are 24 gerbils and 9 hamsters. What is the ratio of hamsters to gerbils?

    A. 1:4
    B. 1:3
    C. 3:8
    D. 2:3
    E. 3:4

15. If the ratio of boys to girls at a dance is 5:3, and there are 65 boys, how many girls must there be at the dance?

    A. 13
    B. 18
    C. 26
    D. 36
    E. 39

16. On a street map, 3/4 of a centimeter represents one kilometer. What distance, in kilometers, is represented by 1-3/4 centimeters?

    A. 1-1/2
    B. 2
    C. 2-1/3
    D. 2-1/2
    E. 2-5/8

17. When filled completely with water, which of these 2 cubes would hold the most liquid?

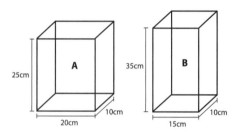

    A. Cube A would hold the most.
    B. Cube B would hold the most.
    C. Both cubes would hold an identical amount.

18. Two hundred percent more than 50 is:

    A. 100
    B. 150
    C. 175
    D. 200
    E. 250

19. Thirty percent of 10 is 10 percent of what number?

    A. 10
    B. 15
    C. 30
    D. 60
    E. 300

20. The price of gum rises from 5 cents to 15 cents. What is the percent increase in price?

    A. 50 percent
    B. 75 percent
    C. 100 percent
    D. 150 percent
    E. 200 percent

21. If $3x = 81$ then $x3 = ?$

    A. 12
    B. 16
    C. 64
    D. 81
    E. 128

22. Which of the following is not a prime number?

    A. 5
    B. 7
    C. 9
    D. 11
    E. 13

23. Find the missing number: 200, 175, 150, _____, 100, 75.

24. What type of triangle has all 3 sides of different lengths and all 3 angles of different sizes?

    A. Scalene
    B. Isosceles
    C. Equilateral
    D. Acute
    E. Obtuse

25. Trums are 5 times as long as Gribs. Bods are 10 times as long as Trums. That means:

    A. Trums are 15 times as long as Bods.
    B. Bods are 15 times as long as Gribs.
    C. Bods are 50 times as long as Gribs.
    D. Gribs are 50 times as long as Bods.

END TEST

ANSWER KEY

1. D
2. B
3. D
4. 855. Add 1, multiply by 1, add 2, multiply by 2, and so on.
5. A
6. C
7. 36
8. 1500. Divide each number by 2.
9. E
10. 113. Primes whose reversal is a different prime.
11. D
12. B
13. 21
14. C
15. E
16. C
17. B
18. B
19. C
20. E
21. C
22. C
23. 125. Subtract 25 from each number.
24. A
25. C

Interpreting Your Score

The chart below will convert your raw score into your estimated IQ score. Simply calculate the number of questions you answered correctly (your raw score) and match it up with the corresponding IQ score on the right.

Raw score	IQ rate
0	<80
1	93
2	96
3	99
4	102
5	105
6	108
7	111
8	114
9	117
10	120
11	123
12	126
13	129
14	132
15	135
16	138
17	141
18	144
19	147
20	150
21	153
22	156
23	159
24	162
25	165

It's important to keep in mind that since this test is not given under controlled conditions and has not gone through rigorous standardizing and normalization, it cannot give a true IQ score. The score given on this test is merely meant to be an indicator of how you might perform on an IQ test. Your obtained score should only be interpreted as a broad estimate of your intelligence.

Chapter 6

High-Ceiling Culture-Fair IQ Test

The high-ceiling culture-fair IQ test is similar to our culture-fair IQ test in that it's primarily designed to test IQ while minimizing cultural and educational biases. The main difference is the difficulty level. The questions are much harder and rely on more spatial ability to solve them than our standard culture-fair test. Like the previous one, this test relies on pictures and images rather than on words and assesses your spatial abilities. The concept of spatial ability consists of several components such as mental rotation, spatial perception, and spatial visualization.

This test features two sets of questions, analog matrices and sequential matrices. They require you to find the pattern in the images and find the box that best completes the pattern. While some may seem simple, there are several "red herrings" in the questions that are designed to purposely distract the test-taker. Finding the correct pattern and extrapolating it to the blank square can get quite tricky.

Number of questions: 25
Time limit: 45 minutes

START TEST

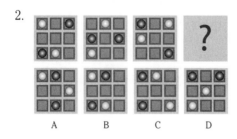

3.

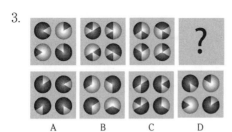

A   B   C   D

4.

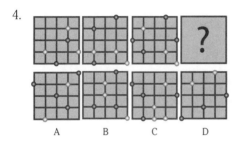

A   B   C   D

5.

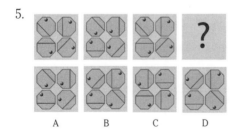

A   B   C   D

6.

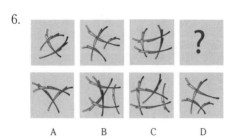

A   B   C   D

7.

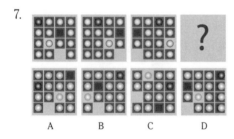

A   B   C   D

8.

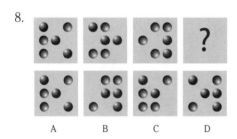

A   B   C   D

9.

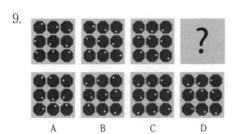

A   B   C   D

10.

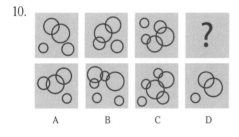

A   B   C   D

11.

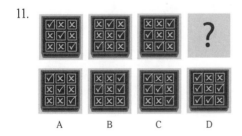

A   B   C   D

12.

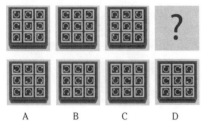

A   B   C   D

13.

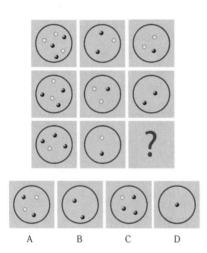

A   B   C   D

14.

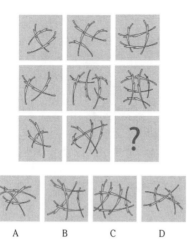

15.

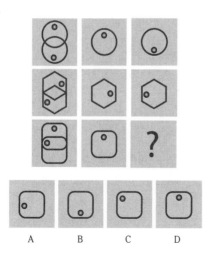

16.

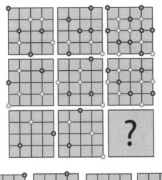

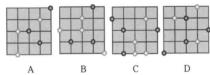

A   B   C   D

17.

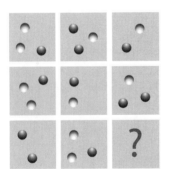

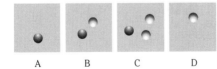

A   B   C   D

18.

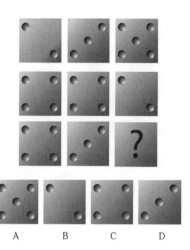

19.

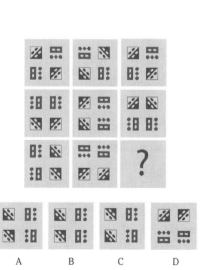

20.

21.

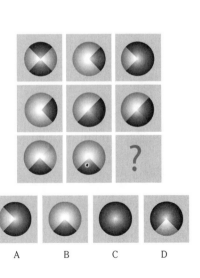

22.

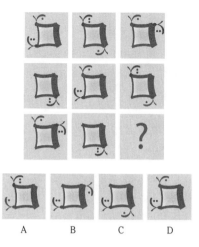

23.

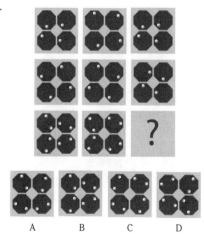

24.

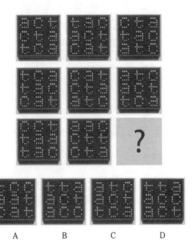

25.

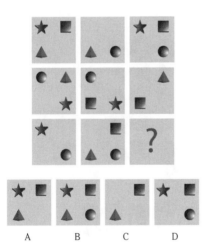

END TEST

ANSWER KEY

1. D
2. A
3. B
4. C
5. A
6. C
7. B
8. A
9. D
10. C
11. A
12. A
13. B
14. C
15. C
16. C
17. C
18. D
19. A
20. D
21. B
22. D
23. B
24. D
25. A

Interpreting Your Score

The chart below will convert your raw score into your estimated IQ score. Simply calculate the number of questions you answered correctly (your raw score) and match it up with the corresponding IQ score on the right.

Raw score	IQ rate
0	<80
1	93
2	96
3	99
4	102
5	105
6	108
7	111
8	114
9	117
10	120
11	123
12	126
13	129
14	132
15	135
16	138
17	141
18	144
19	147
20	150
21	153
22	156
23	159
24	162
25	165

It's important to keep in mind that since this test is not given under controlled conditions and has not gone through rigorous standardizing and normalization, it cannot give a true IQ score. The score given on this test is merely meant to be an indicator of how you might perform on an IQ test. Your obtained score should only be interpreted as a broad estimate of your intelligence.

Chapter 7
High-Ceiling Verbal Intelligence Test

The high-ceiling verbal intelligence test is similar to our verbal intelligence test except for the level of difficulty. The questions are much harder and rely heavily on your ability to notice the relationship between the words.

Verbal intelligence is essentially the ability to use words and language. Those possessing a strong verbal intelligence tend to have highly developed skills for reading, speaking, and writing. This test is designed for those whose first language is English. Take your time, read the questions carefully, and choose the best response. Pencil and paper are allowed, but use of any reference material such as a dictionary, encyclopedia, or thesaurus is not allowed.

Number of questions: 25
Time limit: none

START TEST

1. AILERON is to WING as CAISSON is to:

   A. Bridge
   B. France
   C. Leg
   D. Chicken
   E. North Korea

2. FIBERGLASS is to PLASTIC as FERROCEMENT is to:

   A. Sand
   B. Concrete
   C. Paper
   D. Ship
   E. Sedative

3. ANESTHETIC is to NUMBNESS as ASBESTOS is to:

   A. Construction
   B. Fire retardation
   C. Surgery
   D. Mining
   E. Cancer

4. COURTROOM is to LAWYER as ARENA is to:

   A. Gladiator
   B. Judge
   C. Stadium
   D. Military
   E. Zoo

5. SEDATIVE is to DROWSINESS as ALCOHOL is to:

   A. Thirst
   B. Wine
   C. Dehydration
   D. Fuel
   E. Stomach

6. VACCINE is to VIRUS as SOAP is to:

    A. Medicine
    B. Needle
    C. Wash
    D. Germs
    E. Dish

7. ANTIDOTE is to POISON as DEATH is to:

    A. Vaccine
    B. Life
    C. Funeral
    D. Snake bite
    E. Shots

8. HAND is to _____ as FOOT is to KNEE

    A. Finger
    B. Muscle
    C. Elbow
    D. Arm
    E. Thumb

9. SOPRANO is to CONTRALTO as _____ is to TENOR

   A. Soubrette
   B. Music
   C. Sing
   D. Baritone
   E. Opera

10. COLOMBIA is to BOLIVIA as TUNISIA is to:

   A. South Africa
   B. Libya
   C. Uganda
   D. Mozambique
   E. Senegal

11. ICHTHYOLOGIST is to _____ as BOTANIST is to PLANTS

   A. Marine life
   B. Horticulture
   C. Dinosaurs
   D. Birds
   E. Insects

12. HUMAN is to OMNIVORE as GIRAFFE is to:

    A. Carnivore
    B. Herbivore
    C. Mammal
    D. Primate
    E. Animal

13. LOUISIANA PURCHASE is to _____ as ALASKA is to RUSSIA

    A. Mexico
    B. Spain
    C. France
    D. England
    E. Portugal

14. ARMY is to DEFENSE as FOOD is to:

    A. Digestion
    B. Vegetation
    C. Rations
    D. Nutrition
    E. Taste

15. ODOMETER is to DISTANCE as BAROMETER is to:

   A. Wind
   B. Velocity
   C. Kilometer
   D. Temperature
   E. Pressure

16. EINSTEIN is to HEMINGWAY as PHYSICIST is to:

   A. Writer
   B. Book
   C. Relativity
   D. Painter
   E. American

17. GERONTOLOGY is to AGING as GENEALOGY is to:

   A. Families
   B. Lineage
   C. Birth
   D. Genetics
   E. History

18. BASEBALL is to BAT as POLO is to:

    A. Cricket
    B. Cesta
    C. Mallet
    D. Pelota
    E. Stick

19. REAGAN is to ALI as ALZHEIMER'S is to:

    A. Lou Gehrig's
    B. Hodgkin's
    C. Hansen's
    D. Parkinson's
    E. Forgetful

20. CLAUSTROPHOBIA is to CLOSED SPACES as ACROPHOBIA is to:

    A. Spiders
    B. Insects
    C. Open spaces
    D. Flying
    E. Heights

21. CLEOPATRA is to ASP as JULIUS CAESAR is to:

    A. Knife
    B. Gunshot
    C. King Cobra
    D. Marc Antony
    E. Julius Caesar

22. TADPOLE is to FROG as _____ is to BUTTERFLY

    A. Larva
    B. Caterpillar
    C. Embryo
    D. Egg
    E. Insect

23. FLAMMABLE is to INFLAMMABLE as VALUABLE is to:

    A. Worthless
    B. Cheap
    C. Invaluable
    D. Combustible
    E. Common

24. LION is to ANTELOPE as HAWK is to:

    A. Falcon
    B. Nest
    C. Wings
    D. Mouse
    E. Antlers

25. NORMANDY is to LOIRE VALLEY as ONTARIO is to:

    A. Superior
    B. Ardennes
    C. Dunkirk
    D. Hastings
    E. Quebec

END TEST

ANSWER KEY

1. A
2. B
3. E
4. A
5. C
6. D
7. B
8. C
9. D
10. E
11. A
12. B
13. C
14. D
15. E
16. A
17. B
18. C
19. D
20. E
21. A
22. B
23. C
24. D
25. E

Interpreting Your Score

The chart below will convert your raw score into your estimated IQ score. Simply calculate the number of questions you answered correctly (your raw score) and match it up with the corresponding IQ score on the right.

Raw score	IQ rate
0	<80
1	93
2	96
3	99
4	102
5	105
6	108
7	111
8	114
9	117
10	120
11	123
12	126
13	129
14	132
15	135
16	138
17	141
18	144
19	147
20	150
21	153
22	156
23	159
24	162
25	165

It's important to keep in mind that since this test is not given under controlled conditions and has not gone through rigorous standardizing and normalization, it cannot give a true IQ score. The score given on this test is merely meant to be an indicator of how you might perform on an IQ test. Your obtained score should only be interpreted as a broad estimate of your intelligence.

Chapter 8
Twenty-Minute IQ Test

The twenty-minute IQ test is a timed test consisting of fifty questions. This test is slightly speeded relative to longer IQ tests, so it is sensitive to processing speed and you will need to pay close attention to the time limit if you want to ensure an accurate score.

Number of questions: 50
Time limit: 20 minutes

START TEST

1. If some Greebles are Dribbles and all Greebles are Grobbles, the statement that some Dribbles are Grobbles is:

   A. True
   B. False
   C. Indeterminable from data given

2. The 47th week of the year is in:

   A. December
   B. January
   C. June
   D. November
   E. September

3. If written backward, would the number, "two thousand, four hundred and sixty-nine," be written, "nine thousand, six hundred and forty-two"?

4. Can the word WRISTDRAW be spelled using only the letters found in the word STRAIGHTFORWARD?

5. If written backward, would the number, "two thousand, one hundred and twelve," be written, "two thousand, one hundred and twenty-one"?

6. Is O the seventh vowel of this particular phrase?

7. In the English alphabet, how many letters are there between the letter I and the letter Q?

8. If you remove 7 letters from the word WINDSURFING, can the word GRIND be formed?

9. Rars are 3 times as long as Bofs. Cids are 3 times as long as Rars. That means:

    A. Cids are 6 times as long as Bofs.
    B. Bofs are 6 times as long as Cids.
    C. Cids are 9 times as long as Bofs.
    D. Bofs are 9 times as long as Cids.

10. If some Gannucks are Dorks and all Gannucks are Xorgs, the statement that some Dorks are Xorgs is:

    A. True
    B. False
    C. Indeterminable from data given

11. All Noodles are Joomas and all Noodles are Gundles. All Gundles are Brooles, therefore all Brooles are Joomas.

    A. True
    B. False
    C. Indeterminable from data given

12. Do the words ANGERED, ENRAGED, and GRENADE all use the exact same letters? *yes*

13. IEH is to QMP as FNJ is to:

    A. ZRV
    B. IBF
    C. PKN
    D. PXT
    E. CGB

14. CUP is to COFFEE as:

    A. Tea is to teabag
    B. Straw is to cup
    C. Ice is to freezer
    D. Bowl is to soup ✓

15. SUGAR is to CANE as:

    A. Coffee is to bean ✓
    B. Salt is to sea
    C. Syrup is to maple tree
    D. Milk is to cow

16. EYE is to VISION as:

    A. Finger is to fingerprint
    B. Ear is to sound
    C. Tongue is to taste
    D. Tooth is to pain

17. What word will complete the transformation from FISH to LIST by changing only one letter in the word FISH?

    FISH
    __?__
    MIST
    LIST

18. Do the words RESCUED, RECUSED, REDUCES, SECURED, and SEDUCER all use the exact same letters?

19. The owner of a grocery store hired a young student who was studying cryptology at the university. The student decided to change the prices on some of the goods. Can you figure out his method and determine the cost of the pears?

    PINEAPPLE 14
    POTATOES 12
    FLOUR 8
    MILK 7
    PEARS ?

20. Which word doesn't belong?

    A. EYE
    B. EAR
    C. BOB ✓
    D. OBO

21. What letter doesn't belong? O,T,E,M.

    A. O
    B. T
    C. E
    D. M

22. What word can be added to each of these to create
    3 new words?
    KEEPER SHELF WORM

23. Which of the following is greater than 1/3?

    A. 2/7
    B. 8/30
    C. 6/21
    D. 5/14
    E. 9/31

24. What word can be added to each of these to create a
    3 new words?
    POOR PET FLY

25. If cat is 3-1-20, dog is:

    A. 4-15-7
    B. 3-16-8
    C. 4-16-7
    D. 4-20-6

26. The fire engines arrived at the scene on _____.

    A. call
    B. delay
    C. the double
    D. the highway
    E. time

27. It is rather _____ that her deposition is true.

    A. allegorical
    B. doubtful
    C. illegal
    D. suspicious
    E. unfair

28. The lash of his sharp _____ had them on their guard.

    A. attitude
    B. mouth
    C. razor
    D. sword
    E. tongue

29. It is the last _____ that breaks the camel's back.

    A. bale
    B. bundle
    C. saddle
    D. straw
    E. weight

30. The virtuous will never _____ to vile baseness.

    A. commit
    B. escape
    C. react
    D. stoop
    E. strive

31. The tractor _____ up an acre of trees.

    A. chewed
    B. circled
    C. divided
    D. plowed ✓
    E. pruned

32. Their efforts to stamp out disease were hampered by a _____ of medical supplies.

    A. excess
    B. mound
    C. plague
    D. plethora
    E. shortage ✓

33. Losing her rights made her feel _____ from society.

    A. angered
    B. isolated ✓
    C. relieved
    D. safe
    E. secure

34. In the winter _____ do not fly south.

    A. bees ✓
    B. ducks
    C. geese
    D. sparrows
    E. swallows

35. It takes only one rotten apple in the barrel to _____ the rest.

    A. age
    B. improve
    C. mature
    D. ripen
    E. spoil ✓

36. Nature never rhymes her children, nor makes two men __4__.

    A. alike
    B. brothers
    C. hostile
    D. perfect
    E. poets ?

37. Were the lion to forsake the _____, he would be upon a level with the jackal.

    A. city
    B. food
    C. forest ✓
    D. lakes
    E. village

38. When bad men combine, the good must _____.

    A. disagree
    B. discuss
    C. separate
    D. sleep
    E. unite ✓

39. There is a natural aristocracy amongst humans. The formula for this is _____ and talent.

    A. ancestry
    B. money
    C. politics
    D. virtue
    E. wit

40. His own anger kept him from seeing _____ in others.

    A. anger
    B. goodness
    C. intelligence
    D. sadness
    E. value

41. You can only see _____ at night.

    A. headlights
    B. owls
    C. stars
    D. streetlights
    E. the moon

42. A child _____ in the street what his parents say at home.

    A. covets
    B. lays
    C. repeats
    D. sings
    E. writes

43. It is easier to be critical than to be _____.

    A. correct
    B. free
    C. harsh
    D. popular
    E. safe

44. Thermometer is to temperature as _____ is to time.

    A. clock
    B. dial
    C. hand
    D. hour
    E. minute

45. What we _____ seldom happens, yet what we least expect does.

    A. anticipate
    B. fight
    C. force
    D. most
    E. reason

46. The mind is like the stomach. It is not how much you put into it that counts, but how much it _____.

    A. churns
    B. digests
    C. passes on
    D. retains
    E. swallows

47. No one ever went broke underestimating the _____ of the American public.

    A. brilliance
    B. buying habits
    C. desires
    D. ravings
    E. taste

48. _____ is to without as between is to within.

    A. aside
    B. beyond
    C. close
    D. inside
    E. near

49. Books are to libraries as weapons are to _____.

    A. armories
    B. bullets
    C. guns
    D. soldiers
    E. tents

50. A hearty laugh gives one a _____, while a good cry is a wet wash.

    A. dry cleaning
    B. lift
    C. mile
    D. side ache
    E. sore throat

END TEST

ANSWER KEY

1. A
2. D
3. Yes
4. Yes
5. No
6. No
7. 7
8. No
9. C
10. A
11. B
12. Yes
13. D
14. D
15. C
16. B
17. FIST
18. Yes
19. 8 (Vowels worth 1, consonants worth 2)
20. B
21. C
22. BOOK
23. D
24. HOUSE
25. A
26. C
27. B
28. E

29. D
30. D
31. D
32. E
33. B
34. A
35. E
36. A
37. C
38. E
39. D
40. B
41. C
42. C
43. A
44. A
45. A
46. B
47. E
48. B
49. A
50. A

Interpreting Your Score

The chart below will convert your raw score into your estimated IQ score. Simply calculate the number of questions you answered correctly (your raw score) and match it up with the corresponding IQ score on the right.

Raw score	IQ rate
0	<70
1	70
2	72
3	74
4	76
5	78
6	80
7	82
8	84
9	86
10	88
11	90
12	91
13	92
14	94
15	96
16	98
17	100
18	102
19	104
20	106
21	108
22	110
23	112
24	114
25	116

Raw score	IQ rate
26	118
27	119
28	120
29	122
30	124
31	125
32	126
33	127
34	128
35	130
36	131
37	132
38	134
39	135
40	136
41	138
42	139
43	140
44	142
45	143
46	144
47	145
48	148
49	146
50	150+

It's important to keep in mind that since this test is not given under controlled conditions and has not gone through rigorous standardizing and normalization, it cannot give a true IQ score. The score given on this test is merely meant to be an indicator of how you might perform on an IQ test. Your obtained score should only be interpreted as a broad estimate of your intelligence.

Chapter 9
Ten-Minute IQ Test

The ten-minute IQ test is a timed test consisting of forty questions assessing your verbal, math, and problem-solving skills. This test measures crystallized intelligence, which is the mental skills that are acquired through education, experience, and exposure. Crystallized intelligence is the accumulated knowledge of content and procedural skills (such as how to use the multiplication table). The ten-minute test is slightly speeded relative to longer IQ tests, so it is sensitive to processing speed and you will need to pay close attention to the time limit if you want to ensure an accurate score.

Number of questions: 40
Time limit: 10 minutes

START TEST

1. At the end of a banquet 10 people shake hands with each other. How many handshakes will there be in total?

   A. 100
   B. 20
   C. 45
   D. 50
   E. 90

2. SOLICITOR is to ADVISOR as SYCOPHANT is to:

   A. Blackmailer
   B. Fawner
   C. Flautist
   D. Nobleman
   E. Ruffian

3. Which word is different from the rest?

   A. Capricious
   B. Comical
   C. Playful
   D. Uncanny
   E. Whimsical

4. Pick the number that follows the pattern set by the series: 0, 1, 3, 6, 10, _.

   A. 14
   B. 15
   C. 16
   D. 6

5. Which number does not fit within the following sequence? 1/5, 1/6, 1/8, 1/10, 1/15, 1/30

   A. 1/10
   B. 1/15
   C. 1/30
   D. 1/5
   E. 1/6
   F. 1/8

6. STRANGE is the opposite of:

   A. Familiar
   B. Happy
   C. Obstinate
   D. Peculiar
   E. Similar

7. One orange cost 12 cents. A dozen and a half oranges will cost:

    A. $0.30
    B. $1.44
    C. $1.80
    D. $2.06
    E. $2.16

8. HARSH is the opposite of:

    A. Mild
    B. Severe
    C. Stern
    D. Warm
    E. Weather

9. OBVIOUS is the opposite of:

    A. Apparent
    B. Clear
    C. Conspicuous
    D. Obscure
    E. Visible

10. Indicate the word that is different from the rest.

    A. Hasten
    B. Hurry
    C. Quicken
    D. Run
    E. Rush

11. Which of the following numbers does not fit in with the pattern of the series? 64, 54, 42, 31, 20

    A. 20
    B. 31
    C. 42
    D. 54
    E. 64

12. Which word does not fit in with the rest?

    A. Bronze
    B. Copper
    C. Gold
    D. Platinum
    E. Silver

13. A submarine averages 10 miles an hour under water and 25 miles per hour on the surface. How many hours will it take it to make a 350-mile trip if it goes 2-1/2 times farther on the surface?

    A. 10
    B. 15
    C. 20
    D. 35
    E. 65

14. ACCEPT and EXCEPT are:

    A. Dissimilar
    B. Opposite
    C. Similar

15. A man was given 8 silver dollar coins. However, one of them was fake and he did not know if the fake coin weighed more or less than the other coins. What is the minimum number of weighings that it would take to guarantee him finding the counterfeit coin? Assume a balance scale is used.

    A. 12
    B. 2
    C. 3
    D. 7
    E. Indeterminable from data given

16. What is the opposite of ABDICATE?

    A. Abandon
    B. Attempt
    C. Court
    D. Edit
    E. Occupy

17. If you put the following words into a meaningful statement, what would the last word be?

    A. a
    B. before
    C. comes
    D. fall
    E. pride

18. Which of the following words is related to SOUND as FOOD is to MOUTH?

    A. Ear
    B. Music
    C. Orchestra
    D. Stomach
    E. Throat

19. Tom and Harry caught a dozen fish. Harry caught twice as many as Tom. How many did Tom catch?

    A. 2
    B. 3
    C. 4
    D. 6
    E. 8

20. Which of the following numbers doesn't fit the sequence? 13, 18, 14, 19, 15, 21, 16

    A. 13
    B. 14
    C. 15
    D. 16
    E. 18
    F. 19
    G. 21

21. Which letter does not belong in the sequence? C F J M Q U

    A. C
    B. F
    C. J
    D. M
    E. Q
    F. U

22. If George met Gertrude and Gertrude met Ralph, then the statement that George and Ralph did not meet is:

    A. False
    B. Indeterminable
    C. True

23. If it takes 4 bricklayers an hour to build a wall, how long will it take 5 of them to build the same wall?

    A. 40 minutes
    B. 45 minutes
    C. 48 minutes
    D. 50 minutes
    E. 90 minutes

24. What is the opposite of REPUDIATE?

    A. Crime
    B. Disappoint
    C. Encourage
    D. Endorse
    E. Halt

25. A basketball player shoots 33 percent from the foul line. How many shots must he take to make 100 baskets?

    A. 100
    B. 300
    C. 301
    D. 31
    E. 333

26. If Bob is older than Harry and Harry is older than Sue, the statement that Sue is younger than Bob is:

    A. False
    B. Indeterminable from data given
    C. True

27. What is the opposite of IMBUE?

    A. Clear
    B. Invest
    C. Prize
    D. Tasteful
    E. Texture

28. A bag of coffee beans costs $30 and contains 100 possible servings. However, typical wastage averages 25 percent. For how much must the proprietor sell a cup of coffee to make 150 percent profit per bag?

    A. $0.75
    B. $1.00
    C. $1.25
    D. $2.00
    E. None of these answers are right.

29. Which word does not fit in with the rest?

    A. Cherry
    B. Maple
    C. Oak
    D. Pine
    E. Rosewood

30. If a pair of pants takes 1-1/2 times as much cloth as a shirt, and the total cloth used for the pants and the shirt is $50, how much does the cloth for the pants cost?

    A. $20
    B. $25
    C. $30
    D. $40

31. BOOK is to LIBRARY as PAINTING is to:

    A. Artists
    B. Building
    C. Curator
    D. Easel
    E. Gallery

32. What meaning do the following 2 statements have?

    Don't put all your eggs in one basket.
    Don't count your chickens before they hatch.

    A. Neither the same nor opposite
    B. Opposite
    C. Same

33. Which one of the following numbers doesn't fit the pattern? 5/8, 9/24, 1/4, 2/16, 0

    A. 0
    B. 1/4
    C. 2/16
    D. 5/8
    E. 9/24

34. BISHOP is to CHESS as SOLDIER is to:

    A. Army
    B. Battlefield
    C. Government
    D. Gun
    E. War

35. The following statements:

    Hindsight is always 20/20.
    Can't see the trees for the forest.

    A. Are neither the same nor opposite in meaning
    B. Are opposite in meaning
    C. Are the same in meaning

36. A zoo has some lions and some ostriches. The zoo-keeper counted 15 heads and 50 legs. How many lions were there?

    A. 10
    B. 11
    C. 12
    D. 13
    E. 14

37. A sushi restaurant buys 20 fish for $10 each. The owner knows that 50 percent of the fish will go bad before being served. Each fish creates 10 servings. What price must he charge per serving in order to make a 100 percent profit on his initial investment?

    A. $2
    B. $20
    C. $3
    D. $4
    E. $6

38. The words SURREPTITIOUS and SUSPICIOUS mean:

    A. Neither the same nor opposite
    B. Opposite
    C. Same

39. Three partners venture on a project. They pro-rate their (potential) profits over their $11,000 investment. Sam invests twice as much as Peter. Peter invests 50 percent more than Charlie. If the venture breaks even how much does Charlie get back?

    A. $2000
    B. $2500
    C. $3666.66
    D. $6000
    E. 0

40. The 18th week of the year is in:

    A. February
    B. March
    C. April
    D. May
    E. June

END TEST

ANSWER KEY

1. C
2. B
3. D
4. B
5. F
6. A
7. E
8. A
9. D
10. D
11. D
12. A
13. C
14. B
15. C
16. E
17. D
18. A
19. C
20. G
21. F
22. B
23. C
24. D
25. C
26. C
27. A
28. B

29. D
30. C
31. E
32. A
33. D
34. E
35. A
36. A
37. D
38. A
39. A
40. C

Interpreting Your Score

The chart below will convert your raw score into your estimated IQ score. Simply calculate the number of questions you answered correctly (your raw score) and match it up with the corresponding IQ score on the right.

Raw score IQ rate

A	B
0	<70
1	70
2	72
3	74
4	76
5	78
6	80
7	82
8	84
9	86
10	88
11	90
12	92

13	94
14	96
15	98
16	100
17	102
18	104
19	106
20	108
21	110
22	112
23	114
24	116
25	118
26	120

27	122
28	124
29	126
30	128
31	130
32	132
33	134
34	136
35	138
36	140
37	142
38	144
39	146
40	150+

It's important to keep in mind that since this test is not given under controlled conditions and has not gone through rigorous standardizing and normalization, it cannot give a true IQ score. The score given on this test is merely meant to be an indicator of how you might perform on an IQ test. Your obtained score should only be interpreted as a broad estimate of your intelligence.

Chapter 10
High-Ceiling General Intelligence Test

Our high-ceiling test is similar to our general IQ test but it is designed with much harder questions to produce scores in a higher spectrum than our other tests. This test is composed of two main sections, a verbal section and a non-verbal section. The verbal portion of the test features twenty different types of verbal analogies, which require different methods to solve. The non-verbal portion of the test has two main types of questions; analogic matrices and sequential matrices. For these you need to find the pattern in the images and find the box that best completes the pattern.

The use of pencil and paper is allowed, but electronic devices such as calculators and computers are not, and your score will not be as accurate if they are used.

Number of questions: 40
Time limit: none

START TEST

1. MULCIBER is to MILTON as GLUMDALCLITCH is to:

   A. Swift
   B. Heller
   C. Dickens
   D. Melville
   E. Hardy

2. BLOODY SOCK is to _____ as FESTERING ANKLE SORE is to WINSTON SMITH

   A. Yossarian
   B. Raskolnikov
   C. Pirrip
   D. Prynne
   E. Meussault

3. A TOYOTA is to A WAR AT TARAWA as _____ is to REIGN AT TANGIER

    A. Chariot
    B. Jeep
    C. Kayak
    D. Kiribati
    E. Gilbert Islands

4. KIMBERLITE is to DIAMOND as _____ is to TITANIUM

    A. Hematite
    B. Chalcopyrite
    C. Magnetite
    D. Ilmenite
    E. Chromite

5. CHARLEMAGNE is to PIPPIN THE SHORT as OTTO THE GREAT is to:

    A. Ivan the Terrible
    B. Bismarck
    C. Richard the Fearless
    D. Suleiman the Magnificent
    E. Henry the Fowler

6. KRAKATOA is to INDONESIA as VESUVIUS is to:

   A. Italy
   B. Pompeii
   C. Etna
   D. Sicily
   E. Martinique

7. STAPES is to COCHLEA as CEREBELLUM is to:

   A. Brain
   B. Thalamus
   C. Epiglottis
   D. Ear
   E. Bone

8. SINE is to _____ as MANTISSA is to LOGARITHM

   A. Cosine
   B. Exponent
   C. Trigonometry
   D. Obtuse
   E. Algorithm

9. BORGLUM is to FOUNDING FATHERS as ROEBLING is to:

   A. Russian Revolution
   B. French Resistance
   C. U.S. Civil War
   D. Brooklyn Bridge
   E. Hoover Dam

10. POLLOCK is to WARHOL as REMBRANDT is to:

    A. Dali
    B. Picasso
    C. Manet
    D. Michelangelo
    E. Van Gogh

11. 123 is to ABC as 629 is to:

    A. FBI
    B. FAC
    C. EBK
    D. FBK

12. SMOLT is to SALMON as:

    A. Canary is to bird
    B. Teen is to adult
    C. Orangutan is to ape
    D. Pork is to pig

13. IEH is to QMP as FNJ is to:

    A. ZRV
    B. IBF
    C. PKN
    D. PXT
    E. CGB

14. DEF is to HIJ as NOP is to:

    A. QRS
    B. KLM
    C. TUV
    D. RST
    E. JKL

15. DOB is to BOD as QIP is to:

    A. QIP
    B. PIP
    C. BIP
    D. PIQ
    E. QIQ

16. ZAY is to XDW as VGU is to:

    A. SGT
    B. TGS
    C. TJS
    D. WVU
    E. ZAG

17. HERD is to SHEEP as POD is to:

    A. Wolves
    B. Lions
    C. Cats
    D. Mice
    E. Whales

18. INK is to PEN as:

    A. Blood is to human
    B. Graphite is to pencil
    C. Crayon is to box
    D. Wax is to crayon

19. BOAT is to OCEAN as:

    A. Kite is to air
    B. Worm is to mud
    C. Car is to road
    D. Wheelchair is to cripple

20. PLATELET is to BLOOD as:

    A. Electron is to atom
    B. Brain is to intelligence
    C. Forest is to leaf
    D. Glue is to water

21.

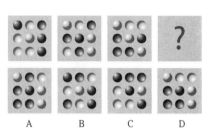

     A   B   C   D

22.

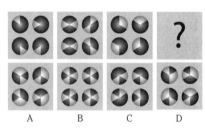

     A   B   C   D

23.

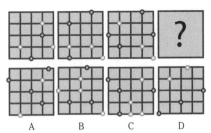

24.

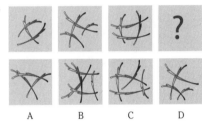

25.

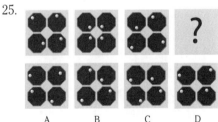

26.

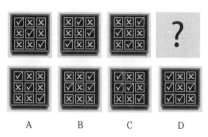

A   B   C   D

27.

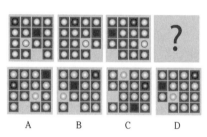

A   B   C   D

28.

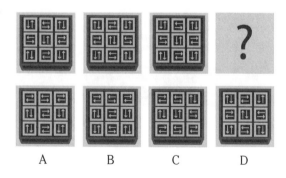

A   B   C   D

29.

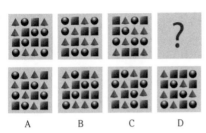

A   B   C   D

30.

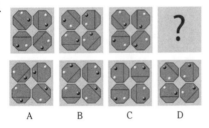

A   B   C   D

31.

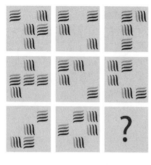

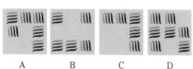

32.

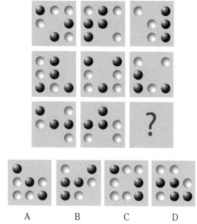

33.

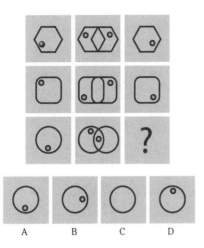

34.

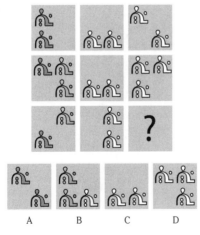

35.

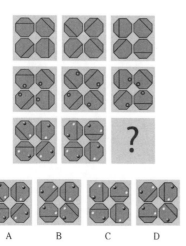

36.

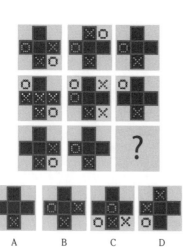

37.

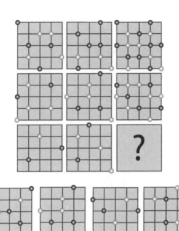

38.

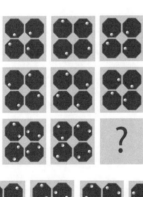

39.

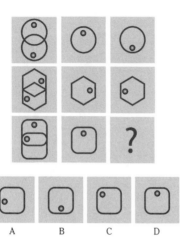

40.

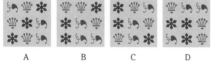

END TEST

ANSWER KEY

1. A
2. B
3. C
4. D
5. E
6. A
7. B
8. C
9. D
10. E
11. A
12. B
13. D
14. D
15. D
16. C
17. E
18. B
19. C
20. A
21. D
22. D
23. C
24. C
25. B
26. A
27. B
28. D

29. B
30. D
31. B
32. D
33. B
34. C
35. D
36. A
37. C
38. B
39. C
40. A

Interpreting Your Score

The chart below will convert your raw score into your estimated IQ score. Simply calculate the number of questions you answered correctly (your raw score) and match it up with the corresponding IQ score on the right.

Raw score   IQ rate

A	B
0	<85
1	87
2	89
3	91
4	93
5	95
6	97
7	99
8	101
9	103
10	105
11	107
12	109

13	111
14	113
15	115
16	117
17	119
18	121
19	123
20	125
21	127
22	129
23	131
24	133
25	135
26	137

27	139
28	141
29	143
30	145
31	147
32	149
33	151
34	153
35	155
36	157
37	159
38	161
39	163
40	165+

It's important to keep in mind that since this test is not given under controlled conditions and has not gone through rigorous standardizing and normalization, it cannot give a true IQ score. The score given on this test is merely meant to be an indicator of how you might perform on an IQ test. Your obtained score should only be interpreted as a broad estimate of your intelligence.

Chapter 11
High-Ceiling Speeded Verbal Analogies Test

This test is designed to stop you before completion. The average test-taker will not complete the test, but it's important to work as diligently as possible. For some questions, figuring out the relationship between the words is only part of the problem. You'll often have to know critical information about historical events, geography, and word etymology in order to arrive at the correct answer.

The verbal analogy question is widely considered to be one of the most accurate measures of general intelligence and of reasoning ability. Those possessing a strong verbal intelligence tend to have highly developed skills for reading, speaking, and writing. This test is designed for those whose first language is English. Take your time, read the questions carefully and choose the best response. Pencil and paper are allowed, but use of any reference material such as a dictionary, encyclopedia, or thesaurus is not allowed.

Number of questions: 50
Time limit: 25 minutes

START TEST

1. _____ is to BRAZIL as POUND is to UNITED KINGDOM

    A. Yuan
    B. Bhat
    C. Real
    D. Peso
    E. Euro

2. PAPER is to TREE as GLASS is to:

    A. Sand
    B. Window
    C. Factory
    D. Lumber
    E. Element

3. CANADA is to NORTH AMERICA as EGYPT is to:

    A. Asia
    B. Africa
    C. Europe
    D. Pacific Rim
    E. Eurasia

4. LEONARDO DA VINCI is to RENAISSANCE as VOLTAIRE is to:

    A. Existentialism
    B. Reformation
    C. Romanticism
    D. Enlightenment
    E. Post Modernism

5. JAI ALAI is to _____ as BICYCLE is to VELODROME

   A. Aztec
   B. Court
   C. Mexico
   D. Track
   E. Fronton

6. CLARINET is to WOODWIND as TRUMPET is to:

   A. Musician
   B. Brass
   C. Instrument
   D. Percussion
   E. Copper

7. MARS is to SATURN as POLARIS is to:

   A. Sirius
   B. North Star
   C. Rings
   D. Jupiter
   E. Galileo

8. LIQUOR is to ALCOHOLISM as FOOD is to:

    A. Overindulgence
    B. Obesity
    C. Calories
    D. Candy
    E. Stomach

9. OSS is to CIA as _____ is to UNITED NATIONS

    A. Treaty of Versailles
    B. League of Nations
    C. House of Commons
    D. Commonwealth
    E. FBI

10. UNICORN is to DODO as GRIFFIN is to:

    A. Horse
    B. Dragon
    C. Pegasus
    D. Great Auk
    E. Icarus

11. SAMUEL CLEMENS is to MARK TWAIN as ERIC BLAIR is to:

    A. John Steinbeck
    B. Huckleberry Finn
    C. George Orwell
    D. Stephen King
    E. Tom Sawyer

12. BIBLIOPHILE is to BOOKS as OENOPHILE is to:

    A. Wine
    B. Foreigners
    C. Perfume
    D. Smell
    E. Masks

13. MAH JONGG is to GO as TILES is to:

    A. Pieces
    B. Dominoes
    C. Cards
    D. Grout
    E. Stones

14. CEYLON is to SRI LANKA as _____ is to ZIMBABWE

    A. Abyssinia
    B. Rhodesia
    C. Africa
    D. Harare
    E. Swaziland

15. MONACO is to FRANCE as _____ is to SOUTH AFRICA

    A. Eritrea
    B. Great Britain
    C. Pretoria
    D. Lesotho
    E. Cape Town

16. SKINNER is to FREUD as BEHAVIORISM is to:

    A. Naturalism
    B. Skinner Box
    C. Psychoanalysis
    D. Socialism
    E. Psychology

17. KEYNES is to DARWIN as ECONOMICS is to:

    A. Naturalist
    B. Creationism
    C. Mathematics
    D. Colonialism
    E. Evolution

18. GUM is to CHEW as BOOK is to:

    A. Read
    B. Paper
    C. Cover
    D. Author
    E. Recipes

19. HAMLET is to MACBETH as MERCHANT OF VENICE is to:

    A. Othello
    B. Romeo and Juliet
    C. Taming of the Shrew
    D. Julius Caesar
    E. King Lear

20. GAVRILO PRINCIP is to ARCHDUKE FERDINAND as GUITEAU is to:

    A. Martin Luther King, Jr.
    B. Charles de Gaulle
    C. Marshall Tito
    D. Lee Harvey Oswald
    E. James Garfield

21. SEATO is to MANILA as LEAGUE OF NATIONS is to:

    A. New York
    B. Precursor
    C. Treaty
    D. Versailles
    E. NATO

22. PAINTER is to CANVAS as LAPIDARY is to:

    A. Gems
    B. Acrylic
    C. Gallery
    D. Appraisal
    E. Pencil

23. PRESIDENT is to WHITE HOUSE as VICE PRESIDENT is to:

    A. Congress
    B. Naval Observatory
    C. Embassy
    D. Private residence
    E. West wing

24. HOBBES is to ENLIGHTENMENT as KIERKEGAARD is to:

    A. Reformation
    B. Existentialism
    C. Romanticism
    D. Creationism
    E. Post Modernism

25. SAN MARINO is to ITALY as _____ is to SOUTH AFRICA

    A. Eritrea
    B. Great Britain
    C. Pretoria
    D. Lesotho
    E. Cape Town

26. SEDATIVE is to DROWSINESS as ALCOHOL is to:

    A. Thirst
    B. Wine
    C. Dehydration
    D. Fuel
    E. Stomach

27. VACCINE is to VIRUS as SOAP is to:

    A. Medicine
    B. Needle
    C. Wash
    D. Germs
    E. Dish

28. NORMANDY is to CHAMPAGNE as ONTARIO is to:

    A. Superior
    B. Ardennes
    C. Dunkirk
    D. Hastings
    E. Quebec

29. SILICON is to ARSENIC as IODINE is to:

    A. Chlorine
    B. Radon
    C. Germanium
    D. Bismuth
    E. Poison

30. GINI COEFFICIENT is to INCOME INEQUALITY as HERFINDAHL INDEX is to:

    A. Opportunity cost
    B. Industry concentration
    C. Economy of scale
    D. Supply and demand curve
    E. General equilibrium

31. NIKKEI is to JAPAN as HANG SENG is to:

    A. London
    B. South Korea
    C. Yuan
    D. Hong Kong
    E. Taiwan

32. ROYGBIV is to COLOR SPECTRUM as PEMDAS is to:

   A. Visible light
   B. Periodic table
   C. Order of operations
   D. Taxonomic hierarchy
   E. Geologic ages

33. METEOROLOGY is to WEATHER as HOROLOGY is to:

   A. Horoscopes
   B. Food
   C. Religion
   D. Shape of the skull
   E. Time

34. GALVANOMETER is to CURRENT as KATHAROMETER is to:

   A. Atmosphere pressure
   B. Thermal conductivity
   C. Electrical resistance
   D. Blood pressure
   E. Radiation pressure

35. ICHTHYOPHOBIA is to FISH as SOMNIPHOBIA is to:

    A. Sleeping
    B. Eating
    C. Sounds
    D. Death
    E. Insects

36. DECOMPRESSION SICKNESS is to THE BENDS as PNEUMOCONIOSIS is to:

    A. Athlete's foot
    B. Morning sickness
    C. Black lung
    D. Lung water
    E. Asthma

37. HARVARD is to MASSACHUSETTS as PRINCETON is to:

    A. Rhode Island
    B. Delaware
    C. New York
    D. New Jersey
    E. California

38. _____ is to DINNER as NOON is to EVENING

    A. Lunch
    B. Afternoon
    C. Night
    D. Snack
    E. Food

39. ENGINE is to CYLINDER as BOOK is to:

    A. Piston
    B. Library
    C. Shelf
    D. Car
    E. Pages

40. ROBBERY is to INCARCERATION as SMOKING is to:

    A. Cigarettes
    B. Lung cancer
    C. Prison
    D. Matches
    E. Tobacco

41. LIGHT BULB is to FILAMENT as WHEEL is to:

    A. Electricity
    B. Road
    C. Spoke
    D. Automobile
    E. Pulley

42. NORTH STAR is to DOG STAR as POLARIS is to:

    A. Orion
    B. Mercury
    C. Ursa
    D. Sirius
    E. Iridium

43. VIENNA is to PRAGUE as WEIN is to:

    A. Praha
    B. Austria
    C. Mozart
    D. Danube
    E. Budapest

44. OIL is to NATURAL GAS as WIND is to:

    A. Sun
    B. Coal
    C. Nuclear
    D. Turbine
    E. Renewable

45. WALES is to UK as POLAND is to:

    A. Ukraine
    B. USSR
    C. EU
    D. Euro
    E. Warsaw Pact

46. GHENT is to PANMUNJOM as SHIMONOSEKI is to:

    A. Maastricht
    B. Hubertusburg
    C. Nanking
    D. Okinawa
    E. Manila

47. 103 is to LOCKERBIE as 007 is to:

    A. James Bond
    B. MI5
    C. England
    D. Sea of Japan
    E. Korean

48. LAMP is to LIGHT as SUN is to:

    A. Dark
    B. Night
    C. Life
    D. Moon
    E. Star

49. FIRE is to SMOKE as POLLUTION is to:

    A. Damage
    B. Garbage
    C. Acid rain
    D. Resources
    E. Environment

50. RGB is to CMYK as DIGITAL is to:

    A. Analog
    B. Print
    C. Color spectrum
    D. ROYGBIV
    E. Electronic

END TEST

ANSWER KEY

1. C
2. A
3. B
4. D
5. E
6. B
7. A
8. A
9. B
10. D
11. C
12. A
13. E
14. B
15. D
16. C
17. E
18. A
19. C
20. E
21. D
22. A
23. B
24. B
25. D
26. C
27. D
28. E

29. A
30. B
31. D
32. C
33. E
34. B
35. A
36. C
37. D
38. A
39. E
40. B
41. C
42. D
43. A
44. A
45. C
46. B
47. D
48. C
49. C
50. B

Interpreting Your Score

The chart below will convert your raw score into your estimated verbal IQ score. Simply calculate the number of questions you answered correctly (your raw score) and match it up with the corresponding IQ score on the right.

Raw score	IQ rate			Raw score	IQ rate
0	<70			26	118
1	70			27	119
2	72			28	120
3	74			29	122
4	76			30	124
5	78			31	125
6	80			32	126
7	82			33	127
8	84			34	128
9	86			35	130
10	88			36	131
11	90			37	132
12	91			38	134
13	92			39	135
14	94			40	136
15	96			41	138
16	98			42	139
17	100			43	140
18	102			44	142
19	104			45	143
20	106			46	144
21	108			47	145
22	110			48	148
23	112			49	146
24	114			50	150+
25	116				

It's important to keep in mind that since this test is not given under controlled conditions and has not gone through rigorous standardizing and normalization, it cannot give a true IQ score. The score given on this test is merely meant to be an indicator of how you might perform on an IQ test. Your obtained score should only be interpreted as a broad estimate of your intelligence.

Chapter 12
Speeded Verbal Analogies Test

This test is designed to stop you before completion. The average test-taker will not complete the test, but it's important to work as diligently as possible. For some questions, figuring out the relationship between the words is only part of the problem. You'll often have to know critical information about historical events, geography, and word etymology in order to arrive at the correct answer.

The verbal analogy question is widely considered to be one of the most accurate measures of general intelligence and of reasoning ability. Those possessing a strong verbal intelligence tend to have highly developed skills for reading, speaking, and writing. This test is designed for those whose first language is English. Take your time, read the questions carefully and choose the best response. Pencil and paper are allowed, but use of any reference material such as a dictionary, encyclopedia, or thesaurus is not allowed.

Number of questions: 45
Time limit: 20 minutes

START TEST

1. CELLO is to VIOLIN as TRUMPET is to:

   A. Viola
   B. Flute
   C. Piano
   D. Harpsichord

2. GAUDY is to OSTENTATIOUS as POVERTY is to:

   A. Misery
   B. Penury
   C. Poorhouse
   D. Hunger

3. REMUNERATIVE is to PROFITABLE as PLOT is to:

   A. Conspire
   B. Entice
   C. Deduce
   D. Respire

4. CREPUSCULAR is to DIM as QUIDNUNC is to:

   A. Testator
   B. Theorist
   C. Quisling
   D. Busybody

5. PLUMB is to VERTICAL as DIURNAL is to:

   A. Horizontal
   B. Diary
   C. Daily
   D. Crooked

6. BLANCHED is to PALLID as REGALE is to:

   A. Entertain
   B. Remain
   C. Contorted
   D. Baked

7. WEALTHY is to INDIGENT as PARSIMONY is to:

    A. Frugality
    B. Ephemeral
    C. Generosity
    D. Abstemious

8. ACCORD is to BREACH as GAUCHE is to:

    A. Clandestine
    B. Graceful
    C. Clumsy
    D. Prolix

9. PLETHORA is to DEARTH as SCARCE is to:

    A. Abundant
    B. Few
    C. Cornucopia
    D. Hardly

10. BIRTH is to TANGIBLE as DEATH is to:

    A. Clear
    B. Certain
    C. Tasty
    D. Abstract

11. FIRE is to SMOKE as BIGOTRY is to:

    A. Racism
    B. Tolerance
    C. Infirmity
    D. Hatred

12. COSTLY is to CHEAP as RESCIND is to:

    A. Refuse
    B. Validate
    C. Parsimonious
    D. Rest

13. PLANT is to SEED as WINE is to:

    A. Sun
    B. Flower
    C. Grape
    D. Liquor

14. HEAT is to FIRE as LIGHT is to:

    A. Sun
    B. Smoke
    C. Dark
    D. Night

15. SUFFOCATION is to AIR as STARVATION is to:

    A. Water
    B. Food
    C. Anorexia
    D. Death

16. SLICE is to LOAF as INGREDIENT is to:

    A. Bread
    B. Bake
    C. Whole
    D. Recipe

17. FAITH is to PRAYER as WORK is to:

    A. Entertainment
    B. Church
    C. Income
    D. Office

18. BRONZE is to ALLOY as IRON is to:

    A. Element
    B. Steel
    C. Silver
    D. Ore

19. CHAFF is to WHEAT as DREGS is to:

    A. Society
    B. Wine
    C. Denizens
    D. Stalk

20. WHOLE is to PART as UNITED STATES is to:

    A. North America
    B. United Kingdom
    C. Okinawa
    D. Texas

21. LIMESTONE is to MARBLE as QUARTZ is to:

    A. Quarry
    B. Watch
    C. Granite
    D. Sedimentary

22. SILO is to BARREL as WHEAT is to:

    A. Wine
    B. Chaff
    C. Staves
    D. Casks

23. SOUND is to TASTE as HEAR is to:

   A. Color
   B. Smell
   C. Food
   D. Ear

24. HOLSTER is to SCABBARD as GUN is to:

   A. Beatle
   B. Sword
   C. Bullet
   D. Armory

25. GRAPE is to APPLE as VINE is to:

   A. Juice
   B. Yard
   C. Pear
   D. Tree

26. INDIA is to PAKISTAN as SPAIN is to:

   A. Cambodia
   B. Portugal
   C. Balearic Islands
   D. Mexico

27. JUNE is to MARCH as DECEMBER is to:

    A. September
    B. August
    C. July
    D. January

28. RAISIN is to PRUNE as GRAPE is to:

    A. Vine
    B. Berry
    C. Plum
    D. Seed

29. SUMMER is to WINTER as NEW YORK is to:

    A. Fall
    B. Sydney
    C. London
    D. Rain

30. STREAM is to RIVER as POND is to:

    A. Brook
    B. Fish
    C. Water
    D. Lake

31. DOG is to CANINE as COW is to:

    A. Bovine
    B. Equine
    C. Feline
    D. Cat

32. SAND is to PAPYRUS as GLASS is to:

    A. Reeds
    B. Stone
    C. Paper
    D. Egyptian

33. HEMINGWAY is to PLATH as WOOLF is to:

    A. Thompson
    B. Walden
    C. Hawthorne
    D. Faulkner

34. NY is to WV as SC is to:

    A. PA
    B. AZ
    C. CA
    D. RI

35. BUILDING is to RAZE as SHIP is to:

    A. Sail
    B. Scuttle
    C. Dock
    D. Moor

36. BASEBALL is to INNING as FOOTBALL is to:

    A. Period
    B. Half
    C. Quarter
    D. Superbowl

37. CADUCEUS is to SCALES as DOCTOR is to:

    A. Justice
    B. Medicine
    C. Sophocles
    D. Lawyer

38. MOAI STATUES is to EASTER ISLAND as STONEHENGE
    is to:

    A. Ireland
    B. England
    C. Scotland
    D. Wales

39. LEXICOGRAPHER is to DICTIONARY as WAINWRIGHT is to:

    A. Wagon
    B. Screenplay
    C. Schooner
    D. Law

40. DISCOMFORT is to PAIN as UPRISING is to:

    A. Anesthesia
    B. Marxist
    C. Revolution
    D. Settlement

41. LANDMARK is to PRESERVING as OPERA HOUSE is to:

    A. La Scala
    B. Singing
    C. La Boheme
    D. Possessing

42. BOOT is to SANDAL as ARTILLERY SHELL is to:

    A. Cannon
    B. Uniform
    C. Gunpowder
    D. Bullet

43. DATUM is to STRATUM as DATA is to:

    A. Strata
    B. Strati
    C. Stratums
    D. Stratus

44. VELLUM is to PAPER as RISOTTO is to:

    A. Papyrus
    B. Italian
    C. Rice
    D. Patty

45. WHEEL is to SPOKE as FORK is to:

    A. Handle
    B. Tine
    C. Road
    D. Plate

END TEST

ANSWER KEY

1. B
2. B
3. A
4. D
5. C
6. A
7. C
8. B
9. A
10. D
11. D
12. B
13. C
14. A
15. B
16. D
17. C
18. A
19. B
20. D
21. C
22. A
23. C
24. B
25. D
26. B
27. A
28. C

29. B
30. D
31. A
32. C
33. A
34. D
35. B
36. C
37. D
38. B
39. A
40. C
41. B
42. D
43. A
44. C
45. B

Interpreting Your Score

The chart below will convert your raw score into your estimated verbal IQ score. Simply calculate the number of questions you answered correctly (your raw score) and match it up with the corresponding IQ score on the right.

Raw score	IQ rate
0	<70
1	70
2	72
3	74
4	76
5	78
6	80
7	82
8	84
9	86
10	88
11	90
12	92
13	94
14	96
15	98
16	100
17	102
18	104
19	106
20	108
21	110
22	112
23	114
24	116
25	118

Raw score	IQ rate
26	119
27	120
28	121
29	122
30	124
31	125
32	126
33	127
34	128
35	130
36	132
37	134
38	136
39	138
40	140
41	142
42	144
43	146
44	148
45	150+

It's important to keep in mind that since this test is not given under controlled conditions and has not gone through rigorous standardizing and normalization, it cannot give a true IQ score. The score given on this test is merely meant to be an indicator of how you might perform on an IQ test. Your obtained score should only be interpreted as a broad estimate of your intelligence.

Appendix A
Glossary of IQ Terminology

Aptitude test: Aptitude refers to a person's capacity to learn, and an aptitude test is designed to predict how well you will perform at something in the future, like in college, or a particular job. An achievement test, on the other hand, is designed to measure how well you did, such as how well you did in high school (the SAT for example).

Cognitive ability test: This type of test is designed to measure a person's intelligence and general mental ability. Modern psychology is moving away from terms like "IQ test" or "intelligence test" and using the more general term cognitive ability test instead.

Crystallized intelligence: There are two main types of intelligence, fluid and crystallized intelligence. Crystallized is the sum of all your learned knowledge that you've developed over time. The capital of the United States, your phone number, etc., are all crystallized intelligence.

Fluid intelligence: Fluid intelligence is the opposite of crystallized intelligence. It's "hard-wired" into your brain and cannot be changed. Solving a visuospatial puzzle is something that would require fluid intelligence. Fluid is considered genetic, while crystallized is learned.

Intelligence: In response to the highly controversial book, *The Bell Curve*, fifty-two of the leading psychologists of the time wrote an open letter to the scientific community—later published in *The Wall Street Journal* in 1994—which I feel gives the best, most thorough definition of intelligence: Intelligence is a very general mental capability that, among other things, involves the ability to reason, plan, solve problems, think abstractly, comprehend complex ideas, learn quickly, and learn from experience. It is not merely book learning, a narrow academic skill, or test-taking smarts. Rather, it reflects a broader and deeper capability for comprehending our surroundings—"catching on," "making sense" of things, or "figuring out" what to do.

Intelligence quotient (IQ): This is a mathematical formula that is defined as the ratio of mental age (MA) to chronological age (CA) multiplied by 100 (thus IQ = MA/CA x 100). For example, if a 15-year-old answers the questions like an average 15-year-old would, the person would have an IQ of 100 (15/15 x 100 = 100).

Appendix B
History of Intelligence Testing

The concept of intelligence testing began with a nineteenth-century British scientist named Sir Francis Galton. Most today recognize Galton's book on hereditary intelligence, *Hereditary Genius*, to be the first scientific investigation into the concept of intelligence.

The first to devise a test to assess human intelligence, however, was French psychologist Alfred Binet. In 1904, the French government commissioned Binet to find a method of differentiating between children who were intellectually normal and those who were inferior. The purpose was to put the inferior children into special schools where they would receive additional schooling. Binet's test was called the Binet Scale and it was at this time that the phrase "intelligence quotient," or "IQ," first appeared.

An American school administrator, H.H. Goddard, found out about Binet's work in France and decided to use his test to screen students for his school. After knowledge of Goddard's use of Binet's test spread across the country, a professor at Stanford, Lewis Terman, worked on revising Binet's test for years. In 1916, Terman published his seminal work, the *Stanford Revision of the Binet-Simon Scale of Intelligence* (also known as the Stanford-Binet), which quickly became the gold standard for intelligence testing in the United States for the next several decades.

When America entered World War I, the U.S. Army was faced with the problem of sorting huge numbers of draftees into various Army positions. To solve this problem, the Army put together an ad hoc committee of the top psychologists in the country to design an intelligence test for new recruits. Lewis Terman was on the Army's committee and they adopted a standard test for all new recruits, which, by 1919, had been taken by nearly two million soldiers. The Army's test put intelligence testing on the map and its popularity exploded shortly thereafter.

After the war ended, many companies began testing their employees and potential employees, and school boards across the country began standardized intelligence testing for all children. By the 1950s, nearly every school district in the country was conducting some form of intelligence testing.

Modern psychology has refined the intelligence test to a degree never thought possible even fifty years ago. Many consider the IQ test not only the most important achievement in the field of psychology, but one of the crowning achievements in modern society. In 1989, the American Academy for the Advancement of Science listed the IQ test among the twenty most significant scientific discoveries of the century along with nuclear fission, DNA, the transistor, and flight.

Appendix C
Resources for Further IQ Testing

Books

Carter, Philip. *The Complete Book of Intelligence Tests.* (John Wiley & Sons, 2005)

Haselbauer, Nathan. *The Mammoth Book of IQ Puzzles.* (Carroll & Graf, 2005)

Herrnstein, Richard. *The Bell Curve: Intelligence and Class Structure in American Life.* (Free Press, 1994)

MacKintosh, N.J. *IQ and Human Intelligence.* (Oxford University Press, 1998)

Sullivan, Norman. *The Big Book of IQ Tests.* (Black Dog & Leventhal Publishers, 1998)

Zenderland, Leila, et al. *Measuring Minds: Henry Herbert Goddard and the Origins of American Intelligence Testing.* (Cambridge University Press; Reprint edition, 2001)

Organizations and Web Sites

Intelligence Theory and Testing
www.indiana.edu/~intell

This site includes biographical profiles of people who have influenced the development of intelligence theory and testing, in-depth articles exploring current controversies related to human intelligence, and resources for teachers.

APA Online
www.apa.org

The American Psychological Association has a wealth of information available online regarding intelligence testing and current leaders in the field.

Uncommonly Difficult IQ Tests
www.eskimo.com/~miyaguch/hard_iq.html

This site is one of the top online destinations, archiving dozens of online tests, and providing numerous links to high IQ societies, the history of IQ, and estimated IQs of historical geniuses.

International High IQ Society
www.highiqsociety.org

This Web site provides standardized online tests, including the *Composite Mental Abilities Intelligence Test—Electronic Edition*.